THE POWER OF ADVERTISING

Ruth Thomson

Franklin Watts
First published in Great Britain in
2017 by The Watts Publishing Group

Copyright © The Watts Publishing
Group, 2017

Credits
Editor: Sarah Peutrill
Designer: Peter Scoulding

HB ISBN 978 1 4451 5516 6
PB ISBN 978 1 4451 5517 3

Printed in China

Franklin Watts
An imprint of
Hachette Children's Group
Part of The Watts Publishing Group
Carmelite House
50 Victoria Embankment
London EC4Y 0DZ

An Hachette UK Company
www.hachette.co.uk

www.franklinwatts.co.uk

THE POWER
OF
ADVERTISING

Ruth Thomson

W
FRANKLIN WATTS
LONDON•SYDNEY

CONTENTS

INTRODUCTION

Take a look around you. Every minute of every day, adverts are never far away. They can be found just about anywhere where lots of people will see them. Outdoors, billboards line busy main roads. Posters are displayed on buses and at bus stops, at rail and underground stations and sports stadia.

You watch commercial breaks in TV shows and before feature films in cinemas. You see adverts every time you open a newspaper or magazine. Online, you see pop-up banner and YouTube adverts. Adverts appear in video games and on your mobile. Your household probably receives direct mail leaflets and catalogues through the letterbox.

In fact, adverts are so much part of modern life, you probably don't bother to think much about them at all. But if you have ever wondered how adverts are made and why some are more eye-catching or memorable than others, this book uncovers some of the answers.

Times Square, New York, is a riot of adverts on billboards and animated LED screens. It is probably the best-known and also the most expensive public advertising space in the world. It is estimated that 39 million people a year see the adverts displayed here.

CHAPTER 1

THE BASICS

However an advert is produced, whether as a printed poster, for TV or as an app on your smartphone, the basic essentials of advertising are the same. Adverts are appealing to you to buy one particular company's product or service rather than another. A successful advertising campaign can have huge public impact and make a company's fortune.

WHY ADVERTISE?

Advertising sends out messages. It is a way of making people aware of products, services or important issues.

The main function of advertising is to draw in consumers and increase sales of an existing product, or to make people aware of new products. Companies not only want consumers to buy their own products, but also to make repeat purchases. Many companies advertise all the time, so that their name or products stand out in consumers' minds – even if people are not about to buy a new product immediately.

The advertisers of this orange juice stress that it comes directly from the orange groves of Florida. This emphasis makes it stand out from other juices that cannot make a similar claim.

Swarovski sells jewellery and watches, which most people do not buy very often. However, the company keeps advertising so that when people are ready to buy a piece of jewellery, they might think about buying a Swarovski product.

SERVICES

Companies that sell invisible products, such as insurance and banking, also advertise. Their adverts have to be especially inventive to engage potential consumers, as there is nothing immediately obvious for them to show.

Illustrating happy parents securely holding onto their child was an appealing way for Prudential to encourage families to take out life insurance.

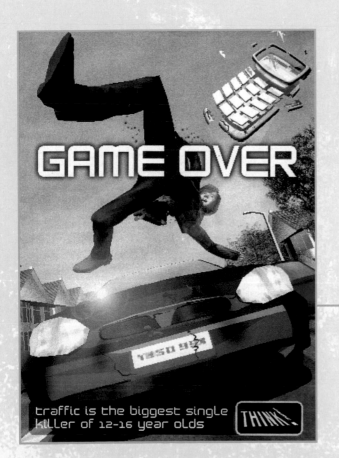

INFORM AND EDUCATE

Charity and public safety adverts are non-commercial. They use the same effective advertising techniques to raise money for causes or to raise awareness of issues and to change people's behaviour.

Public safety advertisements, like this one for road safety, aim to help save lives, to improve health or encourage environmental protection.

BRAND AWARENESS

Another major role of advertising is to promote brands and encourage consumer loyalty to them.

Brands for almost all products – whether cars, computers, chocolate, sports shoes or fast foods – compete with one another for customers. Each one has its own distinctive name, logo and graphics. Advertising helps make sure that potential customers identify a particular brand and trust it. When consumers then go to buy a product, they are more likely to choose one whose brand they recognise.

BRAND LOYALTY

If customers trust and are happy with a particular brand, they are also more likely to buy the same brand again, rather than a brand they don't know. Constant advertising makes sure that a particular brand is the one that consumers will remember the most.

Kellogg's has been the leading brand of ready-to-eat cereals for more than a century. Its founder, K.W. Kellogg, had his signature printed on the front of his whole range of cereals. This branding has not changed for more than a century and is very recognisable.

REBRANDING

How do products remain popular? Rebranding is one answer. This means changing the packaging, the advertising message and the potential consumer market.

ALL CHANGE

Lucozade was launched in 1927 in family-sized bottles. Aimed at mothers looking after unwell children, the adverts suggested that a glass of Lucozade would help children get better.

As the use of Lucozade as a health drink declined, it was rebranded as Lucozade Energy, a drink that helps people live life to the full. Now the brand is modern and energetic, appealing to a wider audience range.

This idea of Lucozade being a drink for sick children was reinforced by including an image of a nurse and a tagline saying that Lucozade was used by doctors and nurses.

SEE FOR YOURSELF

Can you remember what logo or slogan identifies the following brands – without looking them up?

- McDonald's
- Nike
- Coca-Cola
- Apple
- Amazon
- Disney
- Ford
- IBM
- Samsung

BRAND MASCOTS

A good way to make a brand stand out is to associate it
with a memorable character or mascot – animal or human.

Characters create a strong image of a brand in a consumer's mind, distinctive from other brands. Sometimes, actual products, like Michelin tyres and M&M's, are brought to life as mascots with human characteristics. Snap, Crackle and Pop are characters inspired by the noise that toasted rice makes when you pour milk over it. Associating a tiger with Esso petrol was intended to make drivers think that this particular brand of petrol had tiger-like qualities of power and speed.

Characters can also give a face to invisible products, such as insurance.

HUMOUR
Mascots often behave in a humorous way, which makes them both appealing and memorable.

Including an unseen passenger's words, 'I'm sure I heard a roar' emphasises the joke of having a tiger in your tank. To reinforce the idea further, motorists could buy a furry tiger tail to fit on to the boot of their car.

PUT A TIGER IN YOUR TANK!

"BUT GEORGE... I'M SURE I HEARD A ROAR"

Check local listing for time and date.
Watch for the Esso Report on NBC-TV.

NEW POWER-FORMULA ESSO EXTRA GASOLINE BOOSTS POWER THREE WAYS:

1 Cleaning Power! Dirt can clog even a new carburetor in a few months of normal operation—causing hard starting and rough idling. Your very first tankful of New Esso Extra will start to clear away these deposits—in new engines or old—to improve power and mileage.

2 Firing Power! Spark plug and cylinder deposits can cause misfiring, pre-ignition and hot spots. New Esso Extra neutralizes these harmful deposits—to help your engine fire smoothly, to help preserve the power of new cars and restore lost power to many older cars.

3 Octane Power! New Esso Extra has the high octane that most cars now need for full smooth performance without knocking. You'll get *all* these extras with New Power-formula Esso Extra gasoline—it puts a tiger in your tank! *Happy Motoring!*

HUMBLE
OIL & REFINING COMPANY

MAKERS OF FINE ESSO PRODUCTS AND THE ESSO RACING FUELS THAT POWERED A. J. FOYT AND RODGER WARD TO FIRST AND SECOND PLACE IN THIS YEAR'S INDIANAPOLIS 500 MEMORIAL DAY CLASSIC

ESSO

© HUMBLE OIL & REFINING COMPANY, 1964

SEE FOR YOURSELF

Find mascots which advertise:
- home or car insurance
- household goods
- food
- drinks
- sweets

What do they have in common?

Snap, Crackle and Pop have been cartoon mascots for Rice Krispies for more than 80 years. Over time, these gnome-like characters have been redrawn as boys, with more colourful up-to-date clothes, smaller hats, bigger eyes and smaller noses.

The Michelin Man is an illustrated character created entirely of tyres piled one on top of the other. Mascot for Michelin tyres for more than a century, he has been updated from this line drawing into a computer-rendered action hero. In animations, he pulls tyres from his body to help motorists with tyre problems.

THE TARGET AUDIENCE

Adverts were once designed to appeal to as many people as possible. Now they are mostly targeted at particular groups.

When advertisers have a new product to promote, they carefully research the target audience for it and create adverts aimed specifically at that group of people. In creating a suitable advertising campaign, they consider people's age, gender, income, job, education, lifestyle, household size and activities and even their hobbies and the place where they live.

No.1 for sensitive skin*

Persil Comfort

Proven Skin Kindness

*Based on AC Nielsen, MAT, 31st Jan 2016

PRODUCTS

Brands that produce several similar types of products, such as yogurts, cereals, soap or detergents, target specific, different audiences for each one.

Advertisers create distinctive adverts that will appeal to each different group, such as children under 12, teenagers, young men, women with children or older people.

Although this Persil detergent could be used to wash anyone's clothes, this advert specifically targets parents of young babies.

SEE FOR YOURSELF

Find a selection of adverts for a range of the same products, such as deodorant, soap, shampoo, trainers or jeans.

Who do you think is the target audience for each one? How can you tell?

Jeans and jackets from

Cool gear for cool people. Jeans and jackets designed for the tough life. In denim or soft corduroy. Make the scene in a new pair of pants in parallels or flares. Get hooked on any of 13 shades—like red, lemon, petrol blue, loden, wheat,

white, black, rosé and antelope. They're great. They're Wranglers. Available throughout the country. For illustrated brochure, send postcard to: Wrangler Jeans, Dept. N1, Blue Bell, Colwick Industrial Estate, Nottingham, NG4 2DP.

Denim and Corduroy.

Using the pop artwork style and typeface of 1960s' album covers, this Wrangler advert was designed to appeal specifically to teenagers. The colours are bright and clashing, and there is a strong sense of movement and energy.

When targeted at men, adverts often link products to rugged or extreme activities, such as diving, mountaineering, flying a plane or motor racing. The adverts invite men to dream about doing these activities, even if they will never actually do any of them.

If you were racing here tomorrow you'd wear a Rolex.

Sliding through this right-angle bend a Formula One Grand Prix car is travelling roughly 8 yards in a fifth of a second.

So to say Grand Prix racing drivers have a highly developed sense of timing is something of an understatement. Their lives depend on it.

Many of them wear a chronometer they call the best in the world. Its Oyster case is carved out of a solid block of 18 ct. gold or Swedish stainless steel. So much of the work is done by hand, each Rolex Oyster takes more than a year to make.

Jackie Stewart thinks it is time well spent. The Rolex he wears is the Datejust.

ROLEX
OF GENEVA

Write to Rolex, Geneva, Switzerland, for free colour catalogue.

In the 1950s, there was a huge consumer boom, both in America and Europe. As new homes were built after the Second World War (1939–45), people wanted to fill them with fridges, washing machines and other modern time-saving electrical appliances. Manufacturers competed to persuade families that their products were the best.

SEXIST ADVERTISING

During this period, adverts (see right) were often extremely sexist. They assumed that women's only role was as a perfect housewife and mother, who would be thrilled and fulfilled if she owned a new fridge, washing machine, cooker or vacuum cleaner.

The roomy fridge-freezer is stuffed unrealistically full of carefully-arranged food and drink, to show the benefit of having a fridge. The advert implies that mothers did most of the shopping and cooking, showing the woman holding a bag of shopping. By including a smiling child in the picture, the advert implies that a woman who buys a fridge like this one, is a good mother and provider. The daughter is dressed in a child's version of her mother's clothes, as if saying that it won't be long before it's her job to fill the fridge.

ICONIC ADVERTISING

Today, virtually everyone in America and Europe owns a fridge, so there is no need to show what people can keep in one. Instead, this contemporary, high-end fridge has been turned into a shining beacon. It glows from within as well as being in the spotlight.

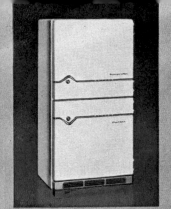

TOOLS AND
TECHNIQUES

In the early 20th century, industrial production took off. Millions of goods were produced for sale. Adverts of the time mainly showed why people might need these goods, stressing their practical uses and durability.

Then advertisers realised that they could sell more products by tapping into people's desires and feelings. Advertisers have developed more and more sophisticated selling techniques to appeal to every type of consumer.

EMOTIONAL APPEAL

A core essential of advertising is to entice people into wanting something, even if they don't actually need it.

Advertisers have long known that our emotional response to an advert has the greatest influence on whether we will buy something. Since there is often no reason why you might buy one product rather than another, adverts try to create a good feeling, perhaps of warmth, happiness, fun or security, that will connect in your mind with the product being shown.

POSITIVE FEELINGS

Many adverts include positive images of fit, attractive people enjoying themselves, spectacular or unspoilt landscapes in perfect weather, happy, rosy-cheeked babies or cuddly animals. These images may have no obvious connection to the product being sold.

A smiling baby in a cuddly rabbit outfit tugs at the heart strings for this brand of washing powder.

A playful puppy and a field of summer flowers are things we might feel good about. They are used here to make us feel good about this particular brand of toilet paper and wipes.

★★★★★

" Goodbye frizz.
Hello gorgeous, sleek hair. "

Lisa, London

People buy shampoo repeatedly, but not always the same brand. They are always on the lookout for one that will make them look and feel their best. Adverts play on people's vanity, like this one promising gorgeous, sleek hair. Including the images of honey and coconut beside the bottles makes people feel that these products are more natural.

NEGATIVE FEELINGS

Charity and public safety adverts often work on fear. Fear creates a sense of urgency, persuading people to take instant action.

WWF is a charity that works to stop climate change and help endangered animals. This advert is persuading us to do something immediate to stop climate change before something terrible happens that affects us personally.

SEE FOR YOURSELF

Look at a selection of adverts for products such as cars, detergents, sweets, watches, soft drinks and toothpaste.

Work out which emotions they are trying to evoke: happiness, warmth, pride, love or envy, guilt, shame, fear or embarrassment?

FUELLING FANTASIES

Many adverts combine idealised images and positive words, constructing a fantasy world for consumers to imagine.

This is particularly true for holiday adverts. The images never show a crowded or stony beach, a rainy day or traffic jams. Instead, they show what many people would consider a dream destination – an empty beach with white sand, a calm sea and blue skies. The only people in the picture are the target audience for these adverts – such as a happy family having fun together, a romantic couple or a lone person sunbathing without any distractions.

WINNING WORDS

The carefully selected verbs on holiday adverts encourage people to *indulge, enjoy, explore, discover, experience* and *absorb.* The accompanying adjectives are all equally enticing.

unspoilt · idyllic · peaceful · fantastic · dreamy · relaxing · gorgeous · unforgettable · amazing · remote · awesome · fabulous · heavenly · enchanting · luxurious

SEE FOR YOURSELF

Look at adverts for different types of holidays – to the seaside, the mountains, cities and different countries.

List the words that describe these places. Which are most frequently used?

Look at the pictures too.
• Do they use a single image to sum up a place or are there several images?
• Do the pictures include landscape, special sites, specific weather and people?
• How do the adverts make you feel?

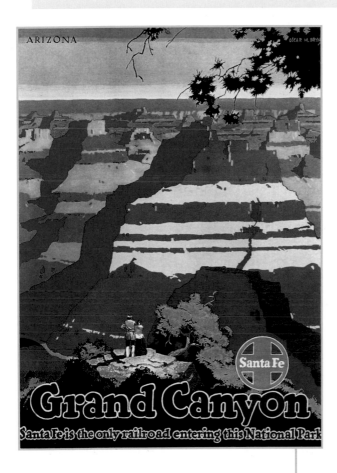

The grandeur and enormity of the Grand Canyon, USA are captured in this vivid illustration. The inclusion of people helps show the scale of the landscape, as well as allowing viewers to imagine themselves in their place.

Photographs of ancient ruins and underwater life have been merged into a single dreamy image. This sums up how Tunisia might appeal to people with very different interests.

MAKING LINKS

Associating a product with something already known to be luxurious, healthy, reliable or innovative can help sell it.

These adverts depend upon consumers already understanding the relevance of the link. Using Paris as a backdrop, for example, is shorthand for romance and sophistication. Advertising luggage in an expensive open-top car suggests the idea of an exciting dream journey.

The Titanic *was nicknamed 'The Ship of Dreams'. Facilities for first-class passengers were the last word in luxury, so linking a brand of soap to it suggests that the soap was also a luxurious product. Since the* Titanic *sank on its maiden voyage, perhaps making this link was not the wild success the advertisers had anticipated.*

Give your skin a healthy start.

New Superdefense. Moisture, antioxidants and SPF…all in our Daily Defense Moisturizer SPF 20. You know what your body needs in the morning. New Superdefense is here to help skin get a great sendoff. Our most complete daily protection in a formula so light and silky it's a pleasure to wear.

clinique.co.uk

CLINIQUE
Allergy Tested. 100% Fragrance Free.

For the health-conscious, a good breakfast is a bowl of yogurt and fruit. The image in this advert implies that using Clinique cream will be as healthy a start for your skin as yogurt and fruit are for your body.

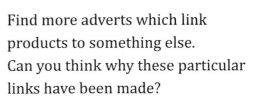

SEE FOR YOURSELF

Find more adverts which link products to something else. Can you think why these particular links have been made?

In the early 1950s, there was intense competition between American car manufacturers. Each year, they produced cars with new engines, longer bodies and stylish interiors. This advert for an Oldsmobile Rocket links it with an actual rocket, seen flying overhead. Since rockets were the very height of technological achievement of the time, this link suggests the Oldsmobile was a cutting-edge car.

CELEBRITY POWER

Linking a product with a celebrity is one of the most successful ways to sell all sorts of products.

The idea of using celebrities, especially film stars, to sell cosmetics, perfume, fashion and jewellery is not new. It began in the 1930s with Max Factor, who provided make-up for Hollywood film stars of the time.

JUST LIKE A CELEBRITY

These adverts, both then and now, imply that if readers use the same products as the stars, then they too could look as attractive as the celebrity. Similarly, if a celebrity is shown with a particular brand of coffee or soft drink, viewers can imagine that, by buying these products, they are sharing the celebrity's experience.

Judy Garland, a major film star in the 1930s and 1940s, featured in many cosmetic adverts.

How many similarities can you find between this cosmetic advert, featuring Halle Berry, and the one above? Compare the models' pose, dress, gaze and background.

Goal by Beckham.
Body by milk.

Heads up. The protein in milk helps build muscle and some studies suggest teens who choose it tend to be leaner. Staying active, eating right, and drinking 3 glasses a day of lowfat or fat free milk helps you look great. So grab a glass and get in the game.

got milk?®
www.bodybymilk.com

thedavidbeckhamacademy.com

Milk consumption in America increased after an ad campaign featuring many celebrities with a milk moustache. Using an image of David Beckham showing off his muscles encouraged consumers to think that milk drinking was healthy, fun and cool.

SPORTS STARS

Sports stars are also widely featured in adverts. Sometimes they promote products related to sports, such as trainers or energy drinks. They also advertise luxury goods, such as expensive watches, mobile phones, cars and luggage, as well as more everyday ones, such as chocolate or coffee.

SEE FOR YOURSELF

Collect adverts that include celebrities. Divide them into three categories – beauty products; luxury goods; everyday products.

Notice the differences between each group of adverts. How do the adverts ensure that you remember the products they are promoting rather than the celebrity?

SHOCKVERTISING

Unlike other kinds of advertising, shockvertising deliberately disturbs or offends people and makes them feel uneasy.

T he idea of shockvertising is not usually to sell anything, but to make people sit up and take notice of an issue – such as racism, smoking, drug abuse, climate change or cruelty to animals. The adverts make their point as powerfully as possible, often with startling images and blunt slogans, showing the worst outcomes.

SHOCKVERTISING EFFECTS

If a shocking advert works, it can change opinions about an issue. But it can also backfire. Smokers often say that anti-smoking adverts do not persuade them to quit, but just make them feel bad. They would prefer positive messages, such as how much money they might save if they quit.

In 1991, Benetton, a clothing company, ran a series of adverts on issues, rather than on its clothes. In this anti-racist advert, a black, white and Asian child stick out their tongues, showing that whatever our ethnicity, our tongues are all the same colour. Adverts like this created a buzz about Benetton and have been long remembered.

The revolting words in this advert, such as 'vomit' and 'excrement', created such feelings of disgust that people changed their behaviour towards flies and food hygiene.

SEE FOR YOURSELF

Find adverts that raise awareness about an issue of your choice. What sort of images and words have the most impact on you?

This powerful advert successfully changed attitudes to wearing fur. Once seen as glamorous, here wearing fur was shown to be associated with animal cruelty, and shamed people who wore it.

This is what happens when a fly lands on your food.

Flies can't eat solid food, so to soften it up they vomit on it. Then they stamp the vomit in until it's a liquid, usually stamping in a few germs for good measure. Then when it's good and runny they suck it all back again, probably dropping some excrement at the same time. And then, when they've finished eating, it's your turn.

Cover food. Cover eating and drinking utensils. Cover dustbins.

The Health Education Council

It takes up to 40 dumb animals to make a fur coat.

But only one to wear it.

LYNX
Fighting the fur trade

If you don't want animals gassed, electrocuted, trapped or strangled, don't buy a fur coat. P O Box 509 Dunmow, Essex Tel: 0371 2016

Everyone loves a bargain. Adverts make the most of this desire by highlighting promotions, such as a half-price sale or special offers, deals and discounts to catch the consumer's eye. Such bargains are usually for a limited time only – perhaps only for a week or just a day – giving a sense of urgency. Consumers are encouraged to think that this might be their very last chance to take up an offer. If they don't buy straightaway, they are made to think they will miss an amazing opportunity.

SPECIAL DEALS

Adverts offering special deals usually feature the price, discount or offer in larger type than the rest of the advert. To make a special offer really stand out, the words may be separated from the rest of the advert, enclosed in a coloured shape, such as a circle, a starburst or an arrow.

All the information in this advert urges shoppers to come and buy at once – with a discount on the price of everything, a time limit on the offer and the instruction to hurry.

SEE FOR YOURSELF

Look at adverts which include bargain offers. Make a list of words and phrases they use to entice potential buyers. What words are used the most often?

New
Best Deal
DISCOUNT

CHAPTER 3

Advertisers choose the words and phrases they use very carefully. They know that particular words can evoke specific feelings. The terms they use are normally glowing, to suggest that a product is the best possible.

CHOICE WORDS

The words that adverts use must trigger immediate interest and a positive response for people to then buy the product.

Since many everyday products, such as washing powders, soap, petrol, yogurts and shampoo, are virtually the same, advertisers choose words that might persuade consumers that one brand is somehow much better than another. They use adjectives and adverbs that suggest superiority – such as *ultimate, unique, utterly, completely, outstanding, ultra, sensational, unbeatable* and *absolutely*.

COMPARISONS

Adverts also often include comparatives, such as *longer-lasting*, or superlatives, such as *best* or *finest*, but without saying what the product is being compared with.

SHORT AND CONCISE

Once, adverts were often very wordy, but now many convey their message in very few words – often not even in complete sentences. Short, snappy words like *magic, great, extra, easy, perfect, rich* and *now* are common trigger words.

The word 'new' is used twice as often as any other adjective in advertising. Why do you think this might be?

HELLO HAPPY SKIN
NEW VITAMIN C
GLOW BOOSTING MOISTURISER

WITH AMAZONIAN CAMU CAMU BERRY RICH IN VITAMIN C

73% SKIN HAS A HEALTHY GLOW*
76% SKIN FEELS ENERGISED**

THE BODY SHOP
VITAMIN C
GLOW BOOSTING MOISTURISER
DULL, TIRED, GRUMPY SKIN

* Based on a consumer-rated study on 102 women
** Based on a consumer-rated study on 106 women

COME IN-STORE FOR YOUR FREE SAMPLE AND JOIN THE #HAPPYSKIN MOVEMENT @THEBODYSHOPUK
In selected stores only. While stocks last.

THE BODY SHOP®

Both the image and the text of this advert combine to make you feel that these ice creams must be better than any others. A gloved hand lifting the silver lid off a silver platter implies these are a posh, expensive dish. The ice creams are described in superlatives, as being the 'finest', the 'most imaginative' and a 'masterpiece'.

SEE FOR YOURSELF

Find all the words in this advert, which might convince people that this product will be of such benefit that they must buy it.

TASTE TINGLING

The words used in food adverts are designed to appeal to your senses, stimulating your craving for a particular food.

Food advertising is mainly for processed foods, such as snack foods, sauces, sweets, fast foods and desserts. The adverts make foods look as delicious as possible, often shown in close-up. Many use warm colours (orange, red and yellow), known to increase appetite. The images are complemented by words using visual terms, such as *golden-brown, crisp* or *plump* or taste words, such as *juicy, chewy* or *fruity*. If an advert is appealing to the health or diet conscious, then adverts will often include words such as *natural, low-fat, fresh, pure* or *free-range*.

The revoluncheon is here

RYVITA
Anything goes

Trust us, the buttery smooth hard boiled eggs mellow the rich smoked mackerel. The tangy pickled beetroot pins the flavours to the spicy bed of rocket leaves on the **Cracked Black Pepper Ryvita Crispbread.**

Although this is an advert for a brand of crispbread, the copy is all about the flavours of the different tasty toppings that you could put on it.

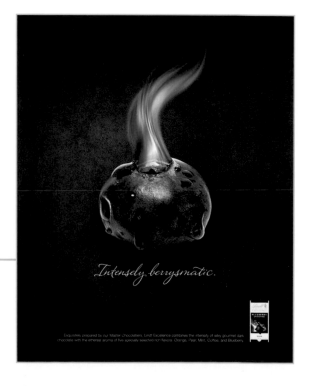

Intensely berrysmatic.

Sometimes, advertisers invent evocative portmanteau words. Combining 'berry' with the last two syllables of 'aromatic' conjures up the taste of chocolate infused with blueberries for this luxury chocolate brand.

Consumers are invited to join in the experience of tasting this biscuit, lured by the superlative 'yummiest' and the tempting taste adjectives, 'creamy' and 'luscious'.

Sometimes, food adverts use statistics to back up their claims – even if, in this case, 100% pleasure is a suggestion, not a fact, like 0% fat.

SEE FOR YOURSELF

Collect food adverts. Divide them into groups which describe foods:
- in visual terms
- in taste terms
- in health terms
- using portmanteau words

Make a list of the words for each group and see how many are repeated.

WORD PLAY

Adverts not only want to attract your interest. They also want to hold your attention for as long as possible.

Using words in surprising and entertaining ways is a technique to make you keep looking at an advert for longer than usual, so that you can work out its message. Advertisers assume that consumers will be smart enough to understand the word play and hope that the jokes are good enough to be memorable.

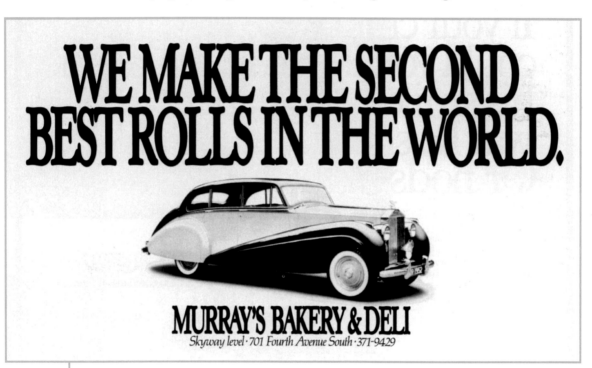

The humour of this advert comes from the pun on the word 'rolls' – using the unexpected image of a Rolls-Royce, a car associated with great luxury, to promote bread rolls. The advert not only makes you look twice, but by linking a Rolls with rolls, the advert also gives the impression that these particular bread rolls are the very best.

SEE FOR YOURSELF

Look for other adverts which use words in different and unusual ways.
Notice whether puns include the brand name of products, to reinforce their message.

d■n't see the point of getting engaged
d■n't see the point of getting
d■n't see the point of
d■n't see the point
d■n't see the
d■n't see
d■n't
d■

A diamond is for...

By taking away a word on each
successive line, the punchline of
this advert for a diamond ring
becomes the very opposite of the
first line. Visually, the diminishing
lines of text form a diagonal with
the ring at its point. This helps
focus your attention on it.

This sophisticated advert for Perrier water gets its message across through a popular
word game. It uses blanks for the missing letters of Perrier and bottle caps for the letter
'o'. It includes watery words, such as 'aqua', 'wet', 'oasis', 'hydro' and 'flows'. Some words
hint at Perrier's French origins, such as 'amour' (love), 'potable' (drinkable) and 'vogue'
(fashionable). Spot a verb and an adjective that describe what Perrier is like.

SLICK SLOGANS

A catchy slogan is an effective way to make an advert stick in consumers' minds. Slogans are often short and simple.

They are usually written in the present tense, which gives a sense of immediacy, but also of timelessness. Some use imperative verbs (such as *go, have, do, feel, use, keep*), making an instant connection to the reader. Alliteration, repetition and rhyme are also useful devices for creating memorable catchphrases.

Clever word play, such as *Tic Tac. Surely the best tactic* or puns, like Zanussi's *The appliance of science,* help slogans stand out. Slogans that include the name of the brand, like those shown here for Heinz and Nestle's KitKat, also help make consumers remember them. Set to music, slogans for TV, YouTube and cinema adverts become catchy jingles.

L'Oréal's slogan 'Because you're worth it' addresses readers directly, making them feel that they are being spoken to not only personally, but also individually.

Here, the slogan is the actual advert. By way of showing the product, overflowing tins of beans substitute for some of the letters of Heinz. Handwritten capital letters (in the same colour as the baked beans) emphasise this rhyming catchphrase.

Nestle's KitKat advert uses repetition of the imperative 'have' to get its message across. The image is a clever joke. This slogan has been in use for more than 50 years.

SEE FOR YOURSELF

Make a list of advertising slogans past and present.
Note which of these techniques the slogans have used.

- present tense
- alliteration
- rhyme
- capital letters
- imperative verb
- word play
- humour
- the brand name

Now and again, adverts have emphasised straightforward facts, rather than using more persuasive language. This appealed to consumers who were jaded by the wild claims of many adverts.

INFORMATION

Chiquita's *How to read a banana* advert gives tips on how to pick the perfect banana. This includes detailed information about the tip, the peel, the ridge and the sugar spots. However, it also gives information about the brand label, implying, as if it is a fact, that Chiquita bananas are more special and better quality than others. Since most people probably take no notice of brands on fruit, an advert like this, with a large image of a single banana, prominent blue sticker and useful facts, makes the brand more memorable.

HONESTY

This uncluttered advert for VW (Volkswagon) cars, was one of the first to use down-to-earth honesty in car advertising, rather than showing aspirational dreams (compare this with the car advert on page 27). It was unusual to have such a bare background, but this makes the viewer focus at once on the car. The text simply stresses the practical benefits of owning a small car. This campaign was hugely successful and helped change Americans' attitudes towards owning small cars.

How to read a banana.

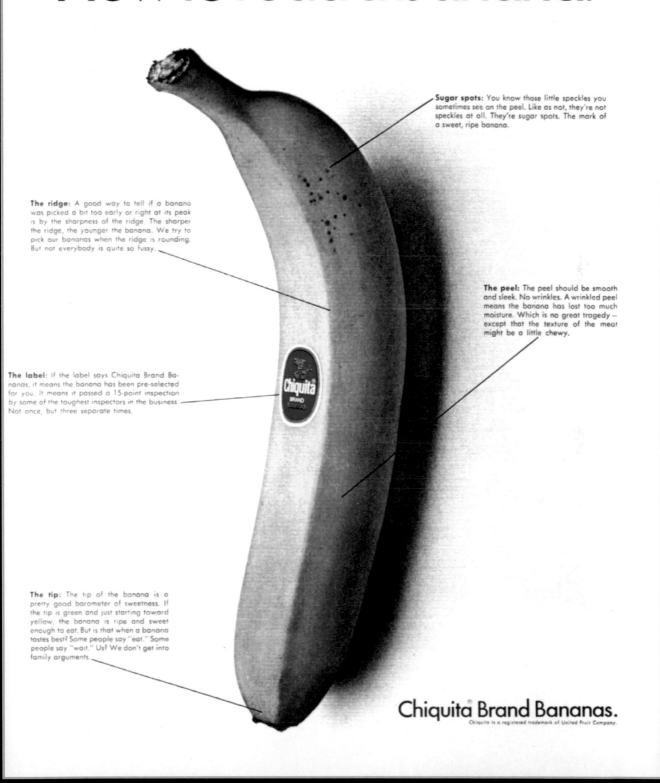

Sugar spots: You know those little speckles you sometimes see on the peel. Like as not, they're not speckles at all. They're sugar spots. The mark of a sweet, ripe banana.

The ridge: A good way to tell if a banana was picked a bit too early or right at its peak is by the sharpness of the ridge. The sharper the ridge, the younger the banana. We try to pick our bananas when the ridge is rounding. But not everybody is quite so fussy.

The peel: The peel should be smooth and sleek. No wrinkles. A wrinkled peel means the banana has lost too much moisture. Which is no great tragedy — except that the texture of the meat might be a little chewy.

The label: If the label says Chiquita Brand Bananas, it means the banana has been pre-selected for you. It means it passed a 15-point inspection by some of the toughest inspectors in the business. Not once, but three separate times.

The tip: The tip of the banana is a pretty good barometer of sweetness. If the tip is green and just starting toward yellow, the banana is ripe and sweet enough to eat. But is that when a banana tastes best? Some people say "eat." Some people say "wait." Us? We don't get into family arguments.

Chiquita® Brand Bananas.
Chiquita is a registered trademark of United Fruit Company.

CHAPTER 4

PICTURE POWER

You look at most adverts for only a few seconds, especially if you are speeding past a billboard in a car, flicking through the contents of a magazine or scrolling on your phone. In a world where we are constantly bombarded with information, adverts with strong visual images are usually the most arresting.

Their strength can come from using stark images, vibrant colours, close-up details, clashes of unexpected images side by side or something shocking, thought-provoking or funny. If an image is powerful enough, it can work by itself with no need for words.

KEEP IT SIMPLE

By using stark, uncluttered images, adverts focus your immediate attention on their product or message.

Adverts like these use bold, contrasting colours and often have large, centred images, like this advert below, which hits you in the eye. Graphic images are often in bright primary colours (red, blue and yellow) and are flat, without any shadows or shading.

Spain was the first country to brand itself with a logo. In 1984, the government wanted to promote Spain as a sunny holiday destination after many years of unrest. Joan Miró (1893–1983), one of Spain's most famous modern artists, painted this strong abstract symbol with the letters of the word 'Spain' in matching colours. He refused any payment, saying this was a gift for the king and the government.

SEE FOR YOURSELF

Find other adverts that use bold images.
What do you notice about the colour combinations they use?

The strong images in this advert play on the conundrum 'Which came first, the chicken or the egg?' The advert puts them both in second place after the courier company DHL. You have to pause a moment to work out the wit – long enough to read the words beside DHL – 'Always first'.

Apple's TV and poster campaign showing silhouettes dancing to music heard through their iPods helped sell millions of these devices. The white iPod, its wires and ear buds stand out against both the black silhouette and the cheerful bright background colour.

PERSUASIVE PICTURES

Purely visual adverts, which have no words apart from the name of the product or brand, can be particularly punchy.

They use universal, easily recognisable images or symbols. A moon signals night-time. Numbers are a symbol of calculation. An elephant symbolises strength. The images in the Lego advert are less immediately obvious, because they have been reduced to essentials. This is deliberate. The advert forces you to use your imagination and spend time working out the joke.

GLOBAL ADVERTS

Purely visual adverts are increasingly common with globalisation. The adverts can be understood anywhere in the world without any need for language translation.

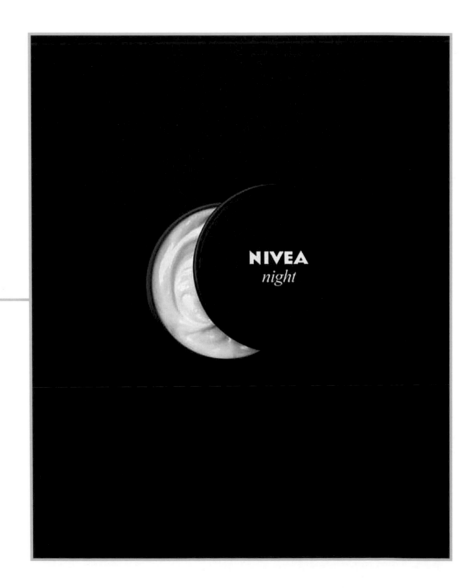

Look at the simplicity of this effective image. The lid of a pot almost disappears on a background of the same colour. It is open just enough to see the cream inside and also doubles as a crescent moon. This reinforces the message that this is a night cream.

A tyre has been drawn as the head of this elephant. Since elephants are known for their power and long life, this advert implies that the tyre has similar qualities.

The colourful array of numbers symbolises the function of the business machines that Olivetti once produced. This makes for a far more striking advert than one showing the actual machines.

This Lego advert is one of a series where tiny brick towers represent cartoon characters, which readers are expected to identify. These included Ninja Turtles and Asterix and Obelix. The colour blocks and different sizes of these towers illustrate the Simpson Family. The giveaway is Marge's high blue hairstyle.

SEEING EYE TO EYE

Adverts showing images of people who stare straight out at you force you to look straight back at them.

Their look draws you in, making you more engaged with the message and so more likely to act – or so advertisers hope.

The first really effective advert using direct eye contact was a British recruiting poster for the First World War (1914–18). Featuring the uniformed head of Lord Kitchener, the Secretary of State for War, with a massive pointed finger, it helped persuade men to sign up for the army. This forceful image inspired a similar poster in America, featuring Uncle Sam.

Lord Kitchener was already a nationally-known figure and war hero when this propaganda advert appeared. His stern eye and pointing finger appear to make direct contact with the individual viewer.

Uncle Sam, the icon of the US government, is dressed in red, white and blue – the colours of the American flag. His frown and accusing finger are even fiercer than those of Lord Kitchener.

COSMETIC ADVERTS

For almost a century, many cosmetic and perfume adverts have used a similar technique. They show a model's face in close-up against a plain background. The model, wearing the product being advertised, looks directly at the viewer. This eye to eye contact helps the reader imagine herself in the model's place.

Cosmetic adverts, like this one, always include samples of the actual products at the base of the advert. This way you will recognise these, when you see them in a shop.

KISSES ON DUTY

"It's amazing!"
Harriet

1000 KISSES LIP TINT

GET A ROYAL FLUSH OF COLOUR.
PLUS A TOUCH OF BALM TO SEAL THE DEAL.
A LIP LOOK THAT STAYS ON DUTY FOR HOURS
AND WON'T LEAVE A TRACE.
FINALLY, KISSES THAT NEVER TELL

RIMMEL
GET THE **LONDON** LOOK

GEORGIA MAY JAGGER wears shade 300 Perpetual Plum

SEE FOR YOURSELF

Find a wide range of adverts for cosmetics, beauty products and perfumes.

Divide them into two groups – one showing models staring straight at you and the other showing models gazing into the distance.

Which gaze do you feel makes for more effective advertising? Can you say why?

Find adverts that show only products, such as nail varnish, lipstick or face cream. Do these adverts seem more or less appealing than those featuring models?

INVISIBLE PRODUCTS

It may seem surprising, but adverts can be just as effective if they do not show the product they are promoting.

These adverts rely on the fact that consumers already know a product or brand. Instead, advertisers want to evoke feelings and thoughts associated with a product, which consumers might remember when they go to buy it.

There's no mention or sign of soap in this Lux advert from the 1900s. It just announces, in an advert within an advert, that Lux won't shrink wool. By showing a field of lambs, whose wool is naturally soft and fluffy, this conjures up the idea that wool will stay in the same state after being washed with Lux.

Norman Rockwell, one of America's most famous illustrators, captures a family's excitement at getting a new car for Christmas, without showing the vehicle. Drawn in to the close-up scene, readers can imagine their own family feeling the same delight at buying the same brand of car.

"Oh, Boy! It's Pop with a new PLYMOUTH!"

EVERYWHERE YOU GO

SWALEDALE, YORKSHIRE   BARNETT FREEDMAN.

YOU CAN BE SURE OF SHELL

In the 1930s, Shell petrol produced a poster series of the British countryside. The romantic images show rolling hills, woods, fields and peaceful villages, offering a quiet escape from the busy cities where most people lived. People could only reach these places by car which, of course, needed petrol. However, roads, cars and petrol stations are nowhere in sight.

SEE FOR YOURSELF

Find other adverts where the actual product is not shown. Think about what feelings and thoughts these adverts are trying to trigger.

THE FREE-RANGE BUTTER Co.   ANCHOR *Butter*

We don't like to boast, but we're the only company making butter from free-range milk.

So, just this once, eh?

Instead of showing butter, milk or even a cow, this advert goes back to basics. It shows in close-up the blades of grass that cows eat. This helps give you the impression that this brand of butter must be connected with nature and freshness.

ARRESTING ARTWORK

Before colour photography, adverts were illustrated. Travel adverts used dramatic images, which have influenced advertisers ever since.

In the 1930s, transport became faster and more comfortable. Companies promoted the speed and luxury of new ships, trains, planes and cars.

A NEW ARTWORK STYLE

Artists used bold shapes, close-ups, blocks of colour and few details. Images on the diagonal suggested dynamism. Images on the horizontal suggested solidity. Words were kept separate, leaving images uncluttered.

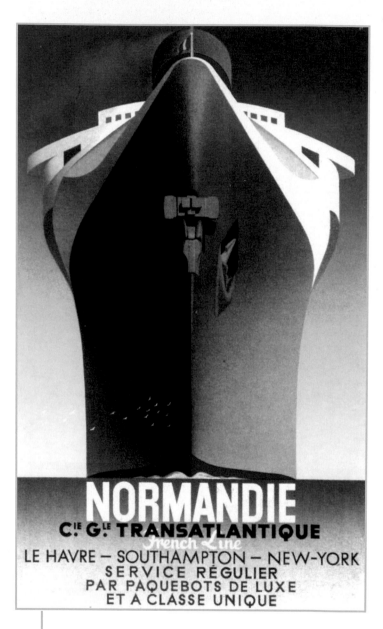

Viewed from under the tracks, this streamlined train seems all the more powerful and fast.

The Normandie was the biggest, most elegant liner of its time. Seen from below, the ship almost fills the poster, exaggerating its size. The tiny seagulls and minute French flag give a sense of scale. The flat sea implies that its journey will be smooth.

This poster links flying with a sunny tropical beach destination.

SEE FOR YOURSELF

Find adverts that entice people to travel by plane, ship, train and car now.

- What main features of each kind of transport do they emphasise?
- Do the adverts include people?
- How do contemporary adverts differ from the ones shown here?

Many 1930s' car adverts depict glamorous wealthy people with their new stylish cars. Notice how the dark shadowy background of skyscrapers helps make the yellow car really stand out.

FOCUS ON ... PLACES

S ince the beginning of mass tourist air travel, airline adverts have often shown an image of a destination. This is a good way of inspiring people to imagine where they might like to go, as well as advertising the airline they might use to get there. Many of these adverts use iconic images, without words (other than the name of the airline), to entice potential passengers.

NEW YORK

The artist of the TWA advert turned the bright neon signs in Times Square, New York (see pages 6–7) into an abstract pattern of brightly-coloured squares and rectangles. The traffic has been reduced to a series of dotted tyre trails and lights are glittering stars. This zingy image conjures up the buzz and excitement of this vibrant city at night.

IRELAND

By contrast, the advert for Ireland emphasises the outdoor pleasures that people can enjoy in green, rolling countryside – golf, fishing, walking, hunting, sailing and horse racing. Buildings and roads scarcely feature, but notice the large images of local animals – horses, fish and a seagull.

SEE FOR YOURSELF

Find wordless travel adverts for other cities or countries.

What do you notice about the images they use for these places? Do they show famous sights or sea and countryside? Do they include people? Do they show only one aspect of a place or contrasting features?

THE ADVERTS

10–11 WHY ADVERTISE?
• Grown, picked and squeezed in Florida: Tropicana orange juice, PepsiCo, 2012, USA. Magazine advert.
• Swarovksi: 2013, UK. Magazine advert.
• Happiness now and their future assured: Prudential PLC, 1950s, UK. Magazine advert.
• Game over: 2002, UK. Department of Transport road safety poster.

12–13 BRAND AWARENESS
• Kellogg's advert: Kellogg Company, 1920s, USA.
• Special K: Kellogg Company, 2004. USA. W.K. Kellogg was an innovative promoter, spending heavily on advertising through newspapers, women's journals and billboards. He even used winning entries in a Kellogg's children's art contest as illustrations for some adverts and gave samples to grocers to give away free to customers who winked at them.
• Lucozade: Lucozade Ribena Suntory Ltd, 1950s, UK. Magazine advert.

14–15 BRAND MASCOTS
• Esso Gasoline: ExxonMobil, 1964, USA. Ad agency: McCann Erickson. Many artists submitted drawings of tigers to the ad agency, which chose the cute, humorous cartoon version by illustrator Bob Jones.
• Snap, Crackle and Pop: Kellogg Company, 1950s, USA. The original gnome-like characters were drawn by Vernon Grant, an American illustrator, who later became known for fairy-tale illustrations.
• Michelin Man: Michelin, 1980s, UK. Magazine advert. Michelin Man (also known as Bibendum) was the idea of André Michelin in 1898. He was first drawn by O'Galop, a French cartoonist, as a man made of tyres, holding a cup of nails and broken glass with the slogan 'Michelin tyres drink up obstacles'.

16–17 THE TARGET AUDIENCE
• No.1 for sensitive skin, Persil/Comfort:

Unilever, 2016, UK. Magazine advert.
• Jeans and jackets from Wrangler: VF corporation, 1960s, UK. Magazine advert.
• Rolex watch: Hans Wilsdorf Foundation, 1968, UK. Ad agency: J. Walter Thompson. Rolex watches were featured in a series of magazine adverts, highlighting extreme activities where time was of the essence, such as flying Concorde, working underwater or yacht racing.

18–19 FOCUS ON ... THEN AND NOW
• smeg: 2015, UK. Magazine advert.
• The Philco: 1950s, USA. Magazine advert.

22–23 EMOTIONAL APPEAL
• As fresh as a daisy: Andrex, Kimberly-Clark Corporation, 2008, UK. Magazine advert.
• Fairy soft, Fairy non-biological washing powder: Procter & Gamble Co., 2000s, UK. Magazine advert.
• Ultimate blends: Garnier, L'Oréal S.A., 2016, UK. Magazine advert.
• Stop climate change, before it changes you: WWF, 2008, Belgium. Ad agency: Germaine, Antwerp. Photography: Christophe Gilbert. The WWF Belgium campaign was designed to lead people to the Reduce Your Climate Impact site. As well as the fish heads appearing in advertising, activists wearing fish heads appeared in public places and on TV shows.

24–25 FUELLING FANTASIES
• Grand Canyon: Santa Fé Railroad, 1949, USA. Billboard poster.
• Tunisia – Here I come: Tunisian National Tourist Office, 2015, UK. Magazine advert.

26–27 MAKING LINKS
• Vinolia Otto toilet soap: Vinolia Otto, 1912, UK. This advert was published only once in the *Illustrated London News*, 6 April 1912. RMS *Titanic* sank on 15 April 1912.
• Give your skin a healthy start: Clinique, The Estée Lauder Companies Inc, 2014, UK. Magazine advert.

• Oldsmobile Rocket (detail): Oldsmobile (General Motors), 1955, USA. Magazine advert.

28–29 CELEBRITY POWER
• Max Factor Hollywood Pan-Cake Make-Up: Procter & Gamble Co., 1945, USA. Model: Judy Garland. Magazine advert.
• Revlon/*Die Another Day*: Revlon Inc, 2002, UK. Model: Halle Berry. Magazine advert.
• Got milk?: California Milk Processor Board, 2006, USA. Ad agency: Goodby, Silverstein and partners. Model: David Beckham.

30–31 SHOCKVERTISING
• Tongues: Benetton Group S.r.l, Italy, 1991. Benetton in-house advertising. Creative control: Luciano Benetton. Photographer: Oliviero Toscani. Realising that there was little difference between one brand and another for his products, Benetton decided to use advertising 'to do something, which is a little more useful'. Toscani's adverts focused on issues, such as birth, death, racism and poverty, which received attention and made the public think.
• This is what happens when a fly lands on your food: 1969, UK. Health Education Council poster.
• LYNX: Respect for Animals: Lynx Animal Welfare Trust, 1986, UK. Yellowhammer agency. Photographer: David Bailey. Bailey was so committed to this cause that he waived his fee for the photoshoot.

32–33 FOCUS ON ... BARGAINS
• Matalan: 2003, UK. Newspaper advert.

36–37 CHOICE WORDS
• Vitamin C glow boosting moisturiser: The Body Shop International plc, 2015, UK. Magazine advert.
• Special Editions, Häagen-Dazs: General Mills, 1987, UK. Ad agency: PUSH International. Magazine advert.
• Finish: Reckitt Benckiser Group plc, 1997, UK. Magazine advert (detail).

38–39 TASTE-TINGLING
• Ryvita – anything goes: Associated British Foods plc, 2016, UK. Magazine advert. Ad agency: W. The paper set behind the food was created by paper artist, Lydia Shirreff, in colours that match the food.
• Berrysmatic: Lindt chocolate, Lindt & Sprüngli AG, 2010, USA. Magazine advert.
• Oreo: National Biscuit Company, 1950s, USA. Magazine advert.
• Sveltesse fat-free yoghurt: Nestlé S.A., 2004, UK. Ad agency: Ogilvy and Mather.

40–41 WORD PLAY
• We make the second best rolls in the world: Murray's Bakery & Deli, 1986, USA. Magazine advert.
• I don't see the point of getting engaged – I do: De Beers, 1986. Magazine advert. In the 1930s De Beers and their advertising agency, N.W. Ayer, created a demand for diamonds. They sold people the idea that a diamond ring was the ultimate symbol of love and romance. People have been buying diamond engagement rings ever since.
• Perrier water: Nestlé S.A., 1990, UK. Ad agency: Ogilvy and Mather. Magazine advert.

42–43 SLICK SLOGANS
• Glam Shine: L'Oréal S.A, 2002, UK. Magazine advert.
• Beanz Meanz Heinz: H. J. Heinz Company, 1967, USA. Ad agency: Young and Rubicon. Slogan writer: Maurice Drake. The whole jingle went, 'A million housewives every day, pick up a can of beans and say Beanz meanz Heinz.' The slogan was in use for 30 years until Heinz decided they wanted to be known for more of their products than beans.
• Have a break, have a KitKat: Rowntree/Nestlé S.A., 1957, USA. Ad agency: J. Walter Thompson.

44–45 FOCUS ON ... FACTS
• Think small: Volkswagen, 1959, USA. Ad agency: Doyle, Dane Bernbach.
• How to read a banana: Chiquita Bananas, 1968, USA. Magazine advert.

48–49 KEEP IT SIMPLE
• Espāna: Spanish Tourist Board, 1984. Artist: Joan Miró (1893–1983). Ignacio Vassallo, Spain's junior minister for tourism, visited Miró in person, to ask him to design the Spanish logo. The slogan chosen to accompany it was 'Spain, diversity under the sun'.

- Always first – DHL: Deutsche Post AG, 2008, USA. Ad agency Jung von Matt/Spree, Berlin. Photographer: Peter Bajer. Magazine advert.
- iPod: Apple Inc, 2003–2005, USA. Ad agency: TBWA/Chiat/Day. Billboard poster.

50–51 PERSUASIVE PICTURES
- Nivea Night Cream: Beiersdorf Global AG, 2005, The Netherlands. Ad Agency: TBWA/Neboko. Photographer: Paul Ruigrok.
- Pirelli tyres: Pirelli & C. SpA, 1955, Italy. Artist: Armando Testa. Testa was an Italian graphic designer and cartoonist who set up his own advertising agency with his wife in 1956. It has now become Italy's foremost agency.
- Olivetti: Olivetti S.p.A, 1949, Italy. Artist: Giovanni Pintori. Pintori was an Italian graphic designer who worked in the advertising department of Olivetti, a typewriter company. His style is known for its simple imagery, geometric shapes and use of basic colours.
- Lego 'Imagine': The Lego Group, 2012, Germany. Ad agency: Jung von Matt.

52–53 SEEING EYE TO EYE
- Britons. Join Your Country's Army!: original image front cover *London Opinion*, 1914, UK. Ad agency: Caxton Advertising. Artist: Alfred Leete. Magazine cover and recruitment poster. Images of Lord Kitchener, Minister of War, appeared on several First World War recruitment adverts and posters.
- I Want You for U.S. Army: Federal Committee of Public Information, 1917, USA. Artist: James Montgomery Flagg. This recruitment poster for the First World War is the best known of the 46 works that Flagg created for the government to help the war effort.
- 1,000 Kisses Lip Tint: Rimmel, Coty, Inc, 2012, USA. Ad agency: Laird and partners. Model: Georgia May Jagger.

54–55 INVISIBLE PRODUCTS
- Lux: Lever Brothers Company, c.1900, UK. Advertising trade card.
- Plymouth Motor Cars, Chrysler Corporation, 1951, USA. Artist: Norman Rockwell. Rockwell's work appeared on 323 covers of *The Saturday Evening Post* over a span of almost fifty years.

- Everywhere you go, you can be sure of Shell: Royal Dutch Shell plc, 1932, UK. Artist: Barnett Freedman. Billboard poster.
- Anchor Butter: Arla Foods UK Limited, 2007, UK. Magazine advert.

56–57 ARRESTING ARTWORK
- New York Central System: 1946, USA. Artist: Leslie Ragan. Ragan was a commercial artist, who specialised in travel posters and calendars. His bold style and unusual angles transformed speeding trains and heavy machinery into heroic objects.
- Normandie Liner: French Line Compagnie Générale Transatlantique, 1935, France. Artist: A. M. Cassandre (real name Adolphe Mouron). Cassandre, a French-Ukrainian, was the first graphic artist to deliberately simplify and dramatise his designs, so they could be read from moving vehicles and by hurrying passers-by. He designed his own typefaces to link with the images, using only capital letters, as he believed that these were easier to read when enlarged.
- Wings over the World: British Airways, 1930s, UK. Artist: unknown.
- Reo Flying Cloud: Reo Motor Car Company, 1930, USA. Magazine advert. Artist: unknown.

58–59 FOCUS ON ... PLACES
- Irish-Aer Lingus: Irish International Airways, c.1965. Ireland. Artist: Philippe Caron. This poster was an advertisement for the newly formed Aer Lingus (Irish International Airline) with its new jet planes and logo – a large shamrock. The artist drew icons for Ireland's attractions and two airliners, one coming from the west and the other from the east, suggesting its jets fly to both Europe as well as Canada.
- Times Square, TWA: Trans World Airlines, 1960, USA. Artist: David Klein. Klein is best known for his many award-winning travel posters for TWA, in the 1950s and 1960s, advertising city destinations and countries. His imagery defines the excitement of the 1960s jet age, when tourism began to take off.

GLOSSARY

advertising campaign a planned series of linked advertisements for a product or brand, shown in different media over one particular time

alliteration the repetition of initial letters or sounds in a sequence of words, e.g. Round and round the rugged rocks, the ragged rascal ran

aspirational strong desire for a higher social standing or standard of living

bargain something offered for sale at a low price

billboard a large board or hoarding used to display advertising posters

brand a product or service that can be identified by its unique and distinctive name, image, design or symbol

comparative an adjective or adverb that expresses a greater quality of something, usually ending in *-er*, e.g. *bigger, taller*

consumer a buyer or customer

conundrum a puzzling question or riddle

emotion a strong feeling or reaction

ethnicity belonging to a group that has a common national or cultural tradition

globalisation the process by which the world has become more interconnected through increased international trade, communications and travel

imperative the form of a verb that gives an order or makes a request

logo a company's emblem or trademark

portmanteau word a new word made by joining together the beginning of one word and the end of another, e.g. *infotainment* is a blend of *information* and *entertainment*

propaganda information used to promote the cause of a government or political cause

pun a joke using either two different meanings of the same word, or words that sound the same, but which are spelled differently (e.g. *hair* and *hare*)

racism prejudice against someone of a different race

rebranding revitalising an established product or brand with a more modern look and feel

sexism prejudice or discrimination, usually against women, on the basis of sex

silhouette an outline drawing of a figure, filled in with black

slogan a memorable phrase or motto

streamlined designed to make movement through the air (or water) as easy as possible

superlative an adjective or adverb that expresses the highest quality of something, usually ending in *-est*, e.g. *finest*

symbol something, such as an elephant, that stands for something else, such as strength

target audience a particular group at which an advert is aimed

INDEX